10 THINGS EVERY CHILD SHOULD KNOW ABOUT

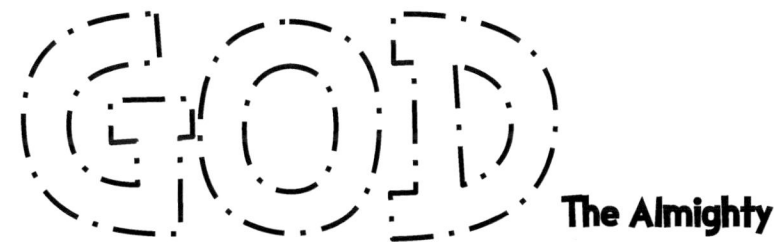
GOD The Almighty

Dr. Heussane

Copyright © 2024 Dr. Heussane

All rights reserved.

ISBN: 9798992001624

www.DrHeussane.com

#1 GOD IS CLOSER THAN YOU THINK.

Imagine yourself all alone in the water. The ship is sinking. No one is there to help, except God Almighty.

If you would like to see God, then feel this way, day and night. God is everywhere, at all times, showing you what is right.

#2 GOD IS THE SOURCE OF ALL LIGHT.

A baby can feel the warmth of the Sun. The light from the Sun shines bright. This gift is from God.

Each thing is like a shadow or light: sun or caused by one. God is the source of all gifts, all life, powering the sun.

#3 EVERYTHING BELONGS TO GOD.

God owns everything, including the oldest thing around. For all things depend on God, even the Sun and the ground.

The Sun's rays are not the Sun, but without it they would die. Without God's care, all things would die, including you and I.

God is the one and only who does not need another. Not even a loving father, son, or any other.

All life, power, knowledge, and everything else are for God. The "richest" of us are poor, we have nothing without God.

#4 GOD HAS THE MOST BEAUTIFUL NAMES

God is not a human or an alien. We say "He" is God but "He" is not a boy or a girl. God created them all.

Call Him "God," "the God, Allah," or simply call upon "Him." Chant God's most beautiful names and do not forget this hymn.

God has no weakness. God is greater than to be imagined or described. God is unique and infinite.

Behind these doors are many things, perhaps infinity. But God is the one who gives them their true identity.

#5 GOD GIVES TO ALL AND LOVES THE GRATEFUL.

God gives to all, even those who do not do what He likes. But God's special love is for the thankful.

God creates each thing to be good but gives people a choice. Those who do the right thing are closer to hearing His voice.

#6 GOD DOES NO EVIL.

God makes every thing good, each has its own purpose. The real evil is when we make bad choices.

We may not know the reason for all things God does each day. But God is pure light, so what He does shines in a good way.

#7 GOD SHOWS US HOW TO GET BETTER.

God shows us what is right inside of us and from the outside too. God sends us the best examples.

One plus one equals two! Be fair, it's the right thing to do. God also sends Prophets with special signs for me and you.

We know many things but very little in the greater picture. Prophets teach us what is beyond our reach.

Prophets confirm what we already know, but so much more. They give instructions based on secrets we should not ignore.

How many true Prophets have you heard about in the past? They would share the same true message, from the first to the last.

Peace be upon him
Moses would challenge the magicians with power from God. Sorcerers who realized their weakness would bow and nod.

True Prophets had the same true message of faith. But some had special instructions for their specific time and place.

Peace be upon him
Jesus would bring the dead back to life with God's permission. As great as he was, loving his Lord was his true mission.

Some Prophets came with special signs that we can see and touch. But some had come with signs that speak to our minds just as much:

A, B, C... God can make miracles with letters like these.
With God's power, it is done, even if you don't say please.

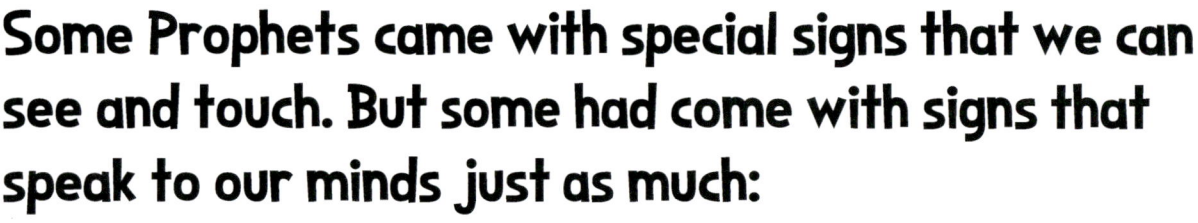

Who is this about?

Let's go find out!

Peace be upon him & his progeny

The last is a mercy for all, including you and me. His miracle is a clear sign for those who wish to see.

This sign is a book challenging the teachers of all time. They can not make anything like it, nothing so sublime.

Sublime? What does that mean?

So beautiful, so awesome. God would not let people be fooled by something so unmatched from someone who is so trustworthy.

#8 GOD MAKES SURE TO PROTECT HIS MESSAGE.

Sometimes people misunderstand the message. And sometimes bad people change it. But God fixes this.

God sends Prophets to teach people and correct their mistakes. God also chooses leaders to protect the truth from fakes.

Each Prophet tells people who the leader after him is.
But if people do not listen, it is their fault, not his.

God protects this superhero to lead a rescue team.
Even if we don't see him, he is real —not just a dream.

#9 GOD LOOKS AT OUR HEARTS, NOT OUR LOOKS.

God is not fooled by how we seem to look on the outside. God loves for us to be beautiful outside and inside.

Why are you doing that? Is your intention a good one? If your intention is sincere, then you've already won.

Make it a habit to do the right thing at the right time.
Fix your innocent mistake and stay away from all crime.

Do not worry, God will forgive you if you try your best.
Good choices lead to good habits, which help you pass the test.

#10 GOD WANTS US TO LOVE HIM THROUGH ALL.

God has all the knowledge and power, so He makes choices with wisdom. He created us with minds to think about why He created things this way.

God made things of many shapes, sizes, colors and flavors. Each and every can help us see His beauty and favors.

Sometimes we see things that have turned ugly. Maybe because we are not seeing the bright side? Or it may be because of someone's bad choices.

But what is broken reminds us of the One who can heal. God wants us to love Him through all — that is how we should feel.

www.ingramcontent.com/pod-product-compliance
Lightning Source LLC
Chambersburg PA
CBRC090058100526
44582CB00013B/174